WHAT IS A
Fable?

ROBYN HARDYMAN

Britannica®
Educational Publishing

IN ASSOCIATION WITH

ROSEN
EDUCATIONAL SERVICES

Published in 2014 by Britannica Educational Publishing (a trademark of Encyclopædia Britannica, Inc.) in association with The Rosen Publishing Group, Inc.
29 East 21st Street, New York, NY 10010

Distributed exclusively by Rosen Publishing.
To see additional Britannica Educational Publishing titles, go to rosenpublishing.com

First Edition

Britannica Educational Publishing
J.E. Luebering: Director, Core Reference Group
Anthony L. Green: Editor, Compton's by Britannica

Rosen Publishing
Hope Lourie Killcoyne: Executive Editor
Nelson Sá: Art Director

Library of Congress Cataloging-in-Publication Data

Hardyman, Robyn.
What is a Fable?/Robyn Hardyman. — First Edition.
     pages cm. — (The Britannica Common Core Library)
Includes bibliographical references and index.
ISBN 978-1-62275-200-3 (library binding) — ISBN 978-1-62275-203-4 (pbk.) — ISBN 978-1-62275-204-1 (6-pack)
1. Fables — Juvenile literature. I. Title.
PN980.H37 2014
398.2 — dc23
                                                                                                2013022568

Manufactured in the United States of America.

CONTENTS

What Is a Fable?

A fable is a short story that teaches a moral, for example, not to be greedy or to think we are smarter than we really are.

Various countries often have similar fables where the moral is the same, but the setting and characters are different.

The fable about a mouse rescuing a lion teaches that different creatures can be great friends.

The characters in a fable are animals or objects that come to life and act like humans. The same animals are used over and over in fables because they behave in a certain way. For example, foxes are smart and wolves are fierce. The animals' behavior helps to tell the moral of the tale.

A **moral** is a lesson in how to behave well.

In the fable about the fox and the crow, the fox tricks the crow into giving up its food.

Why Are Fables Told?

Around the world, people have told fables to teach others how to behave. They wanted to pass on what they had learned about the best way for people to live happily. People used characters and places they knew well in their fables.

STORYTELLERS

The *Jatakas* from India are fables about the Buddha. The stories were kept alive by word of mouth for hundreds of years before being written down.

Statue of Buddha

Over time, people wrote down fables. In ancient Greece, around 2,500 years ago, a man named Aesop collected together fables. Today the collection is called *Aesop's Fables.* The fables have been translated into many languages and are known all around the world.

In Thailand, storytellers told the *Ramakien,* which was based on the Indian *Jatakas.*

Themes in Fables

Fables teach us a lesson. The stories show us how human beings behave well or badly. They show us our weaknesses, such as being greedy, lazy, or too confident. The characters that behave badly lose out. This teaches us to behave well.

Foxes are usually sneaky characters in fables. Sometimes they are too confident.

8

Many fables from different cultures teach similar lessons. For example, fables about one small creature saving the life of another big creature teach that size is not the same as power. Fables about people who wish for more but end up with nothing teach us not to be greedy.

Confident means to feel very sure of yourself and your ability to do things.

Roosters are often boastful characters in fables.

Fables Retold

Now that we know what fables are and why they are told, let's read and compare some wonderful fables from around the world.

The Fox and the Cat

This myth was written down by the ancient Greek storyteller Aesop.

One day, a fox and a cat were walking together. The fox was boasting about how smart he was.

"I know a hundred tricks for escaping from my enemies!" he said.

"I know only one trick for that," said the cat, "but it works for me."

Just then, they heard the sound of hunters and their dogs.

Compare means to look at two or more things to see how alike or different they are.

The cat quickly ran up a tree and hid.

"This is my trick," she said. "What are you going to do?"

The fox could not decide which of his tricks to use. He thought of one, then of another. While he was thinking about the tricks, the dogs caught him and he was killed.

It is better to have one plan that works than a hundred that you cannot depend on.

The cat is wiser than the fox because she acts quickly to save herself.

The Fish That Were Too Clever

This fable comes from India.

Two fish and a frog lived in a pond. One evening, the creatures heard some fishermen talking about coming to fish in the pond the next day.

"What shall we do?" asked Ekabuddhi, the frog. "Should we leave the pond?"

"If they come back, I can protect us," said the first fish, Sahasrabuddhi. "I understand many paths through the water."

The second fish, named Satabuddhi, agreed. "In the water, intelligent understanding will find a path."

STORYTELLERS

This fable is from a collection called the *Panchatantra,* which was printed more than 1,500 years ago.

The fish thought they were smart, but the frog was smarter.

The frog disagreed. "I have only one understanding, and it is telling me to flee." And he left the pond.

The next day, the fishermen returned. They spread their nets on the water. The fish swam one way, and then another, but they were caught and killed.

The frog saw them and said, "Those fish with many ideas are dead but I, with one idea, am still alive."

Let's Compare

Both *The Fox and the Cat* and *The Fish That Were Too Clever* have the same moral—in a time of danger it is better to have one clear plan that works than many plans that might work.

The hounds catch the fox because he is too busy deciding which of his many tricks to use.

The stories are different in their settings and characters. The Greek fable is set in a wood. The characters are a fox, a cat, and hunters with dogs. The Indian fable takes place in a pond. The characters are two fish, a frog, and fishermen. The names of the animals in the second story are typical of the beautiful names in Indian culture.

In both stories the lives of the animals are at risk. The animals that boast about being smart do not survive. The animal that acts quickly, with a simple plan, survives.

Risk means something that could be dangerous. **Survive** means to continue to live; to avoid being killed.

The Tortoise and the Hare

This is another tale from the ancient Greek storyteller Aesop.

One day, a hare was boasting of his speed.

"I have never yet been beaten," he said. "I challenge anyone here to race me."

A tortoise accepted his challenge.

"What a joke!" exclaimed the hare. "You're just a slow tortoise!"

"Do not boast until you have beaten me," the tortoise replied. "Let's race."

The tortoise just keeps going, slowly and steadily.

The hare raced ahead, then stopped. Thinking he was sure to win, he lay down to take a short nap. The tortoise grew tired, but he kept going. When the hare woke up, he saw the tortoise ahead of him, near the finish line. He raced with all his speed, but he could not catch up. The tortoise won the race.

Slow and steady wins the race.

STORYTELLERS

This fable is also in the collection of a Frenchman named Jean de La Fontaine. He wrote his fables in the 1600s.

The Race Between Turtle and Frog

This fable comes from the Sanpoil Native Americans.

In the race between Turtle and Frog, everyone bet that Frog would win. Turtle asked for three days to let his friends know about the race. He had a secret way to finish first, so he bet his back against Frog's tail that he would win. Frog agreed. When the race began, Turtle was given a head start.

STORYTELLERS

The Sanpoil lived on the Sanpoil River in Washington State.

In fables, turtles and tortoises are always slow and steady.

Frog stood around, taking more bets. Finally, he set off. The racecourse was very uneven. Each time Frog looked up, he saw Turtle disappear in a valley ahead of him. He hurried, but he did not overtake him. Finally, he saw Turtle cross the finish line and win. He had to give up his tail. It had taken six turtles to beat him (that was Turtle's secret plan), but Frog lost.

In real life, tadpoles have to lose their tails before they can become frogs.

Frogs lose their tails as they grow into adults.

Let's Compare

The Tortoise and the Hare and *The Race Between Turtle and Frog* have a similar plot—a slow animal races against a fast animal, and wins.

The tortoise wins because he keeps going while the hare stops to rest, but the turtle wins because he cheats. His friends complete parts of the race for him by hiding in the valleys.

STORYTELLERS

The Pueblo and Ojibwa Native Americans have stories like *The Race Between Turtle and Frog.*

The morals of the stories are different. The Aesop story teaches that if we keep trying we will be rewarded. The Sanpoil story teaches that we must not be foolish and too confident.

In the Sanpoil story, the six turtles hide in the hollows of the uneven ground to do their own parts of the race. The story shows how being smart and hiding to outwit your enemy was probably important to the Sanpoil people.

Some Native Americans lived in tepees, such as these in Washington State.

Brer Rabbit and Brer Lion

This well known fable comes from the southern United States.

Brer Lion was a pushy creature who told all the animals around him what to do. One day, he decided to eat one of each kind of animal.

Brer Rabbit decided to make himself look weak and ill to stop Brer Lion from eating him. He said to Brer Lion, "I know I'm not much of a mouthful, but I'm willing to be eaten. I wish I was as big and fat as the creature I just saw."

"Take me to him," ordered Brer Lion, who wanted a bigger meal.

Brer means brother.

Brer Rabbit took Brer Lion to a spring. Looking into the water he said, "Here he is! Let's run away, he's so big!"

Brer Lion leaned over the water, and saw a big creature. Wanting to eat it, he threw himself into the water. Brer Lion could not get out, and drowned.

Brer Rabbit went happily home to his family.

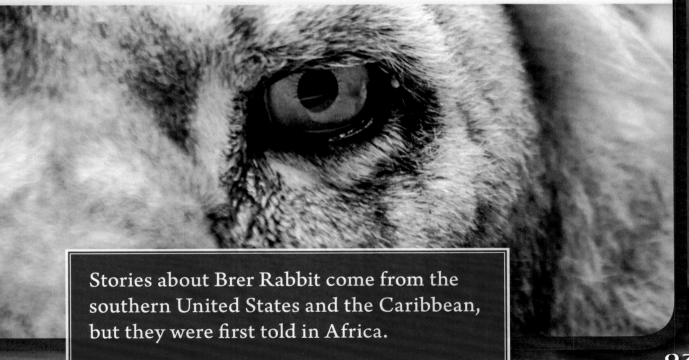

Stories about Brer Rabbit come from the southern United States and the Caribbean, but they were first told in Africa.

The Tiger and the Fox

This fable comes from Pakistan, where there once were many tigers.

A tiger lived in a forest with many foxes and jackals*. Every day, he ate a fox or a jackal. When it was Fox's turn to be eaten, he went to the tiger and said, "Sir, I have come to be eaten. But did you know another tiger has come to live in your country?"*

> **Jackals** are wild animals that look like dogs.

"Where?" roared the tiger. "Show him to me! We cannot both live here!"

The fox led the tiger through the forest to a well. The tiger leaned over and saw the face of a tiger in the water. He leaped in to attack him, and drowned.

The fox went home and told the jackals what he had done. They rejoiced that the tiger was dead.

Once again, a mighty animal is fooled by a smarter one. The moral of the fable is not to want too much power.

Let's Compare

In both *Brer Rabbit and Brer Lion* and *The Tiger and the Fox*, a powerful and greedy animal is tricked by a smart, smaller one. The big animal dies, and the smaller animal escapes from being eaten.

The moral of both stories is the same, too. The lion and the tiger are foolish to want to beat their

The forests of Pakistan are the perfect setting for a fable about tigers.

rivals. They are also too stupid to know that the faces they see in the water are their own **reflections**.

The setting of the second story tells us about the culture it comes from. In Pakistan, there was plenty of forest for tigers to live in. People were afraid of them. They would have liked a story where a tiger was tricked and killed.

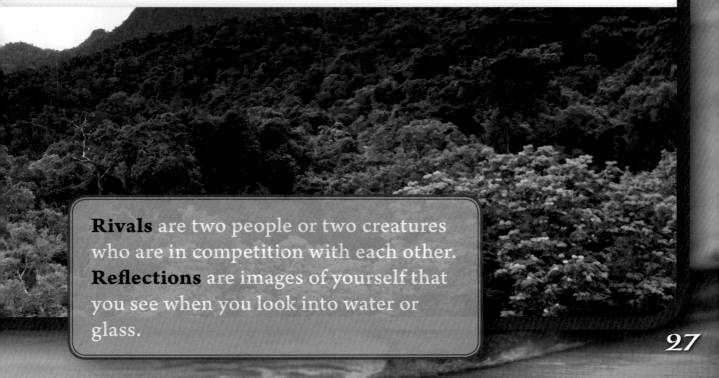

Rivals are two people or two creatures who are in competition with each other. **Reflections** are images of yourself that you see when you look into water or glass.

27

Write Your Own Fable

Are you ready to write your own fable? Here are some simple steps to help you start:

1. Choose your lesson or moral: This is the focus of any fable. You could choose one from the stories in this book or invent your own.

2. Pick a setting: This is the location for your fable. It can be in your own culture or from a different part of the world. Will it be set in the present day or in the past?

3. Find your characters: In a fable these are always animals. They usually talk. They behave in typical ways. For example, foxes are cunning.

4. Sketch out your fable: Make a "map" of the story, showing the start, middle, and end. Keep the plot simple. Include your moral at the end.

5. Write and rewrite! Write your fable, then read it through and change anything you do not like.

Finished? Read your fable to a friend, or one of your family members. Send it in an e-mail to your teacher or a member of your family. You could even post it onto your family's website or blog.

Think about the typical behavior of the animal characters you choose for a fable.

accepted Agreed to do something.

bet To agree with someone that you will receive money or another prize if you choose the correct winner of a race or game.

boasting Showing off to others about something.

Buddha A religious leader who is the founder of Buddhism.

challenge To ask someone to race against you.

characters The people or animals in a story.

cheats Does something (such as playing a game) dishonestly.

cultures The customs and traditions of a group of people.

cunning Sly or smart and crafty.

depend To rely on something or someone.

greedy To want more than you actually need.

hollows Valleys.

Jatakas A collection of fables from India about the Buddha.

Ojibwa A tribe of Native Americans.

Panchatantra A collection of fables from ancient India.

plot What happens in a story.

Pueblo A tribe of Native Americans.

pushy Bossy.

racecourse The route taken in a race.

Ramakien A story from Thailand that is based on the Indian Jatakas.

rewarded Given something good, such as praise or a prize, for doing well.

Sanpoil A tribe of Native Americans.

setting The place where a story happens.

tadpoles Baby frogs.

tepees Tentlike structures in which some Native Americans lived.

translated Changed words from one language into another.

well A hole in the earth where one can get water.

Books

Daily, Don. *The Classic Treasury of Aesop's Fables*. Philadelphia, PA: Running Press Kids, 2007.

Fujikawa, Gyo. *Fairy Tales and Fables*. New York, NY: Sterling, 2008.

Hansen, Doug. *Aesop in California*. Berkeley, California: Heyday, 2013.

Hoberman, Mary Ann. *You Read to Me, I'll Read to You: Very Short Fables to Read Together*. New York, NY: Little, Brown Books, 2013.

Rosen, Suri. *How to Tell a Fable*. New York, NY: Crabtree Publishing Company, 2011.

Websites

Due to the changing nature of Internet links, Rosen Publishing has developed an online list of Websites related to the subject of this book. This site is updated regularly. Please use this link to access the list:

http://www.rosenlinks.com/corel/fable